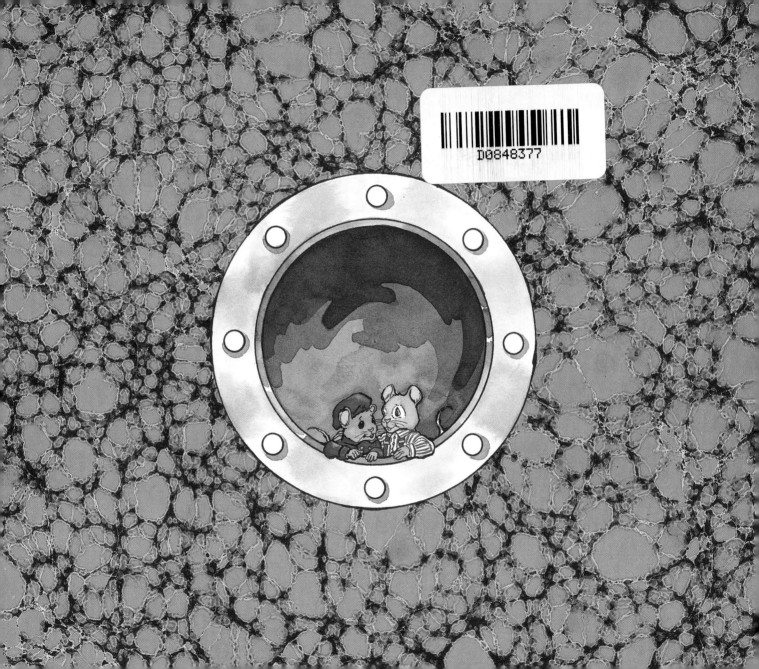

THE
NEW!
CHRISTOPHER
CHURCHMOUSE
ADVENTURES

HIGH ADVENTURE IN PARIS

2 Timothy 3:15 – "And that from a child thou hast known the holy scriptures, which are able to make thee wise unto salvation through faith which is in Christ Jesus."

WRITTEN BY BARBARA DAVOLL
Pictures by Dennis Hockerman

MOODY

Dedicated to our grandson, Jordon Jeffrey Davoll,
born March 13, 1993, to Jeffrey Jon and Deanne Davoll

"I have no greater joy
than to hear that my children walk in truth."
3 John: 4

MOODY PRESS CHICAGO © 1999 by BARBARA DAVOLL AND DENNIS HOCKERMAN

All Scripture quotations, unless indicated, are taken from the *Holy Bible:*
New International Version. NIV. Copyright © 1973, 1978, 1984
by International Bible Society. Used by permission of Zondervan Publishing House.
All rights reserved.

Printed in the United States of America

Dear Diary,

   I just found out where the boat is going. To France! Lukas and I have met a French mouse. His name is Pierre. He is the pet mouse of the French Chef who cooks in the boat kitchen. He is going to show us the sights in Paris. We are having an exciting time. But I do miss my Mama and Papa.

                    Christopher

"Christopher, look! Is that be France?" asked Lukas in his strange way of speaking. The little mouse stood on the deck of the ship that had been their home on the long journey from America. He pointed across the water to a strip of land.

"I believe you're right," Christopher agreed excitedly.

*"Oui, oui!"** [wee] cried the French mouse Pierre. "Oui" was the French word for *"yes."*

Christopher and Lukas had met Pierre on the boat. He was the pet of the French chef on board their ship. Pierre stood jauntily beside them, wearing a red French tam and a beautiful black jacket. He carried a cane with a gold top, which he twirled in his paw.

*"OUI" IS PRONOUNCED "WEE."

"You different look without your tall chef's hat," Lukas said.

"*Oui!* This is my French hat. We call it a tam," Pierre explained. "Frenchmen are always well dressed. We will have a grand time in Paris while the boat is docked. Now we must go ashore and catch a train to take us the rest of the way."

Before long, the two mice were walking down the streets of Paris with Pierre. Their eyes were wide. There was so much color everywhere. On nearly every corner were ladies with flower carts, selling any color of flower you can imagine.

After a feast at a small table in the back room of a restaurant, Pierre took the mice to his apartment. They would spend the night there. Just before bedtime, Pierre told them some of the wonderful history of France. The mice fell asleep dreaming about palaces, kings, queens, and French soldiers.

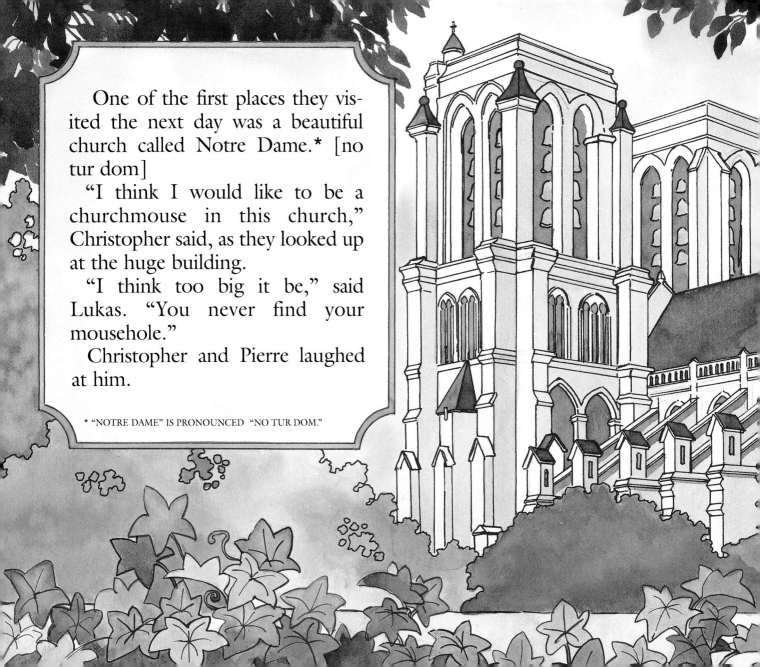

One of the first places they visited the next day was a beautiful church called Notre Dame.* [no tur dom]

"I think I would like to be a churchmouse in this church," Christopher said, as they looked up at the huge building.

"I think too big it be," said Lukas. "You never find your mousehole."

Christopher and Pierre laughed at him.

* "NOTRE DAME" IS PRONOUNCED "NO TUR DOM."

"Come, little friends," invited Pierre. "Let us go inside. You must see the beautiful windows and hear the bells ring."

The mice scrambled after Pierre and entered the church as people passed through the great wooden doors.

"Ohhhh," whispered Christopher. He turned around and around, staring at the beauty about him.

"This wonderful be!" Lukas cried, when he saw a large, round window with the sun sparkling through it. "How they find all those colors?"

"That is called a stained-glass window," explained Pierre. "Those colors are really little pieces of glass all put together in a lovely design."

"Pierre, come look at this stairway. Where do it go?" Lukas asked next. He had found some narrow steps that went so far up he could not see the top.

"Ah, my little friend, you have found the steps to the bell tower," Pierre answered. "Soon the bell ringer will begin to ring the many bells up in the tower."

"Christopher and Lukas see bells ring?" asked Lukas.

"I don't know if – well, maybe it will be all right," agreed Pierre. He knew that visitors usually weren't allowed in the bell tower.

Three little mice won't be noticed, he thought. Besides, he knew a mouse who lived in the tower. *Perhaps I will get to see my old friend.*

Pierre led the way up the bell tower steps. At the top, everywhere the mice looked they saw all sizes of bells hanging from the rafters. Some were small, but most of the bells were huge.

"Take a good look around, boys," said Pierre. "We mustn't be up here when the bells ring. They will be so loud it will hurt your ears. We don't have much time. I'm going to see if I can find my old mouse friend who lives up here. When I get back, we must leave."

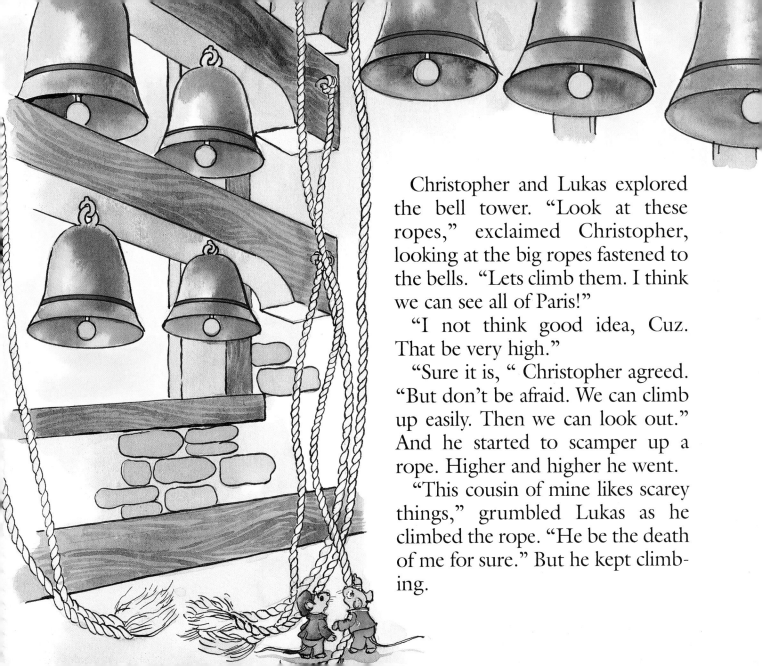

Christopher and Lukas explored the bell tower. "Look at these ropes," exclaimed Christopher, looking at the big ropes fastened to the bells. "Lets climb them. I think we can see all of Paris!"

"I not think good idea, Cuz. That be very high."

"Sure it is, " Christopher agreed. "But don't be afraid. We can climb up easily. Then we can look out." And he started to scamper up a rope. Higher and higher he went.

"This cousin of mine likes scarey things," grumbled Lukas as he climbed the rope. "He be the death of me for sure." But he kept climbing.

Just then, they heard Pierre from down below. He was squeaking his loudest squeak. Another mouse was squeaking too. "Christopher! Lukas! Come down from there. That is very dangerous!"

But Christopher and Lukas were too far above them to hear what they said. The mice boys just waved and kept on climbing. Christopher reached his bell first. When Lukas reached his bell, it began to move! He looked over at Christopher, who was hanging on his rope, looking up into a bell.

"Christopher, my bell is moving!" Lukas screeched.

Suddenly all of the bells were moving, and their big clappers began to sound. The little mice held on for their lives as the bells moved faster and faster and the sounds rang louder and louder. Christopher and Lukas were thrown from one side to the other. They clung frantically to their ropes.

The bells continued to ring, and the sound was deafening. The mice really thought this would be the end of their lives. They knew they could not hold on much longer.

Down below, Pierre and his friend were running around in a panic. What could they do to help?

Suddenly Pierre had an idea. He had been watching the bell ringer run about between the bell ropes, pulling first one rope and then another. Pierre whispered his idea to his old friend, and then they raced across the floor to the bell ringer. They jumped up onto his shoes. Then they started running up and down his legs. The bell ringer started to giggle as the mice tickled his legs. He giggled so much that he had to stop ringing the bells.

Very slowly the bells began to slow down. *Bong! Bong!* Then a long pause. *Bong!* And another *Bong! Bong!* The ringing sound no longer was hurting their ears. Pierre and his friend kept on tickling the bell ringer. He rolled on the floor, trying to get away.

"Stop, you mice! I never heard of mice doing this. You have ruined my bells. Never before have my bells not finished their ringing. Stop, I say!" he screamed, swatting at them with his hands.

Pierre and his friend jumped down from the man's legs. The other mouse went off to the safety of his mousehole. Pierre hid behind some bell ropes. He looked up anxiously at Christopher and Lukas, who were still swaying slowly.

The bell ringer was very upset. He could lose his job over this. *Who can believe mice doing such a thing?* he grumbled. When he got to his apartment in the church, he fixed himself some very strong coffee.

The bells stopped swaying, and the mice were no longer dizzy. As Christopher and Lukas slowly climbed down, Pierre met them. They were safe.

"I'm sorry, Lukas," Christopher said, when they reached the floor. "I shouldn't have suggested we do such a dangerous thing."

"Indeed it was dangerous," Pierre agreed. "But you did not know better."

"Yes, I did," insisted Christopher.

"You see, Pierre, I am a church-mouse. I live in a church. It is not big and fine like this one, but it is a church. And we have a bell tower. I have often wanted to climb up the ropes to the bell. But Mama and Papa have warned me not to do that. It doesn't matter where I am—in America or in France. I should obey my parents."

"Well, that is a very good thing to do, I am sure." Pierre nodded.

As they walked along, Christopher explained how he and his family heard a lot of teaching from the Bible in his church. He was surprised to hear that Pierre had not heard much about Bible teaching.

Lukas was listening. "I'm glad your church not be so big as Notre Dame," he said thoughtfully. "Mama and Papa will be more at home there."

"Are you too tired to see any more of Paris?" Pierre asked.

Lukas yawned, but he said, "Let's see some more!"

"We will see just a few more sights," Pierre said. "Come quickly, before it gets dark." And he hurried ahead of them in his excitement to show them his city.

As they scurried along, they passed a great park with lovely grass and water fountains.

"What be *that*, Pierre?" squeaked Lukas, pointing. A crowd of people was standing around a huge ball of brightly colored cloth. The ball was attached to a big basket with ropes.

Pierre stopped. "That, my dear friends, is a hot-air balloon. Have you never seen one?"

The mice boys' eyes were wide. "No, never," Christopher cried. "Oh, please, may we see it closer?"

"Of course. We must," Pierre said.

The mice squeezed between the people's feet and looked up. They felt overwhelmed by the size of the balloon.

"Come," Pierre suggested. "We can climb up the ropes of the balloon and see it better."

The two mice followed their French friend up the lines that were fastened to the balloon's basket. And they *could* see everything much better from their perch on the ropes.

"See! There on the ground are the men who will go up in the balloon," Pierre said. And looking down, the mice could see all the provisions the men were taking for their trip.

"The balloon, where it go?" asked Lukas

"I'm not sure," Pierre admitted. "Often they just take visitors for a short ride."

"Let's look at the stuff down in the basket," suggested Christopher. The mice climbed down and ran around in the bottom of the basket. They saw coils of rope and other 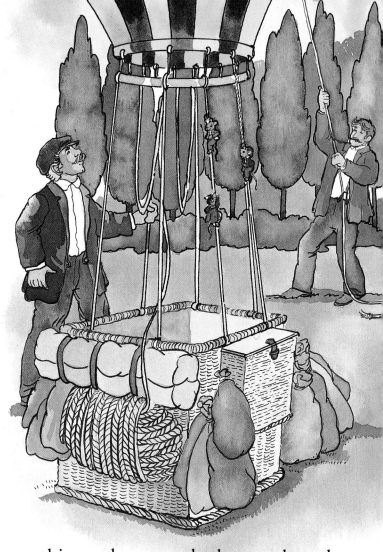 things the men had put aboard. Everything was so interesting.

Suddenly Christopher called, "Hey, Pierre, where's Lukas?"

"I thought he was with you," squeaked Pierre.

Christopher turned around and smiled. "I found him," he whispered. Lukas, tired out from his bell adventure, had fallen sound asleep behind a coil of rope.

When Pierre saw the sleeping mouse, he realized how tired they all were. "I think I could stand a little nap, too. How about you, Chris?"

Christopher looked at Pierre with tired eyes and nodded. Paris could wait. And before you could say "catnap," all three mice were asleep in the basket.

THROUGH THE MOUSEHOLE

Does this French adventure make you wish you could visit France? Do you ever wonder about people in other countries?

In many ways, all people are the same. Most people in the world love their children and families. And most people work hard to make a living. But some do not have the advantages others do. Pierre did not have the advantage of living in a church as Christopher did. So he had never heard much about the Bible.

Wasn't it special that Christopher got to tell him what he had heard in his church? Christopher was like a missionary, who tells people about God.

Although there are many beautiful churches around the world (like the one that Christopher and Lukas saw), some of them do not teach the Bible. So millions of people do not know about God's love for them and Jesus' death on the cross for their sins.

Have you ever thought about how much God loves the world? John 3:16 says, "For God so loved the **world**, that He gave His only begotten Son, that **whoever** believes in Him should not perish, but have eternal life."

Perhaps you can tell others about God's love. Then you can be a missionary, even while you are a child. And maybe you want to pray about being a missionary when you are older. God's plan is for all to know about Jesus. Will you tell them?

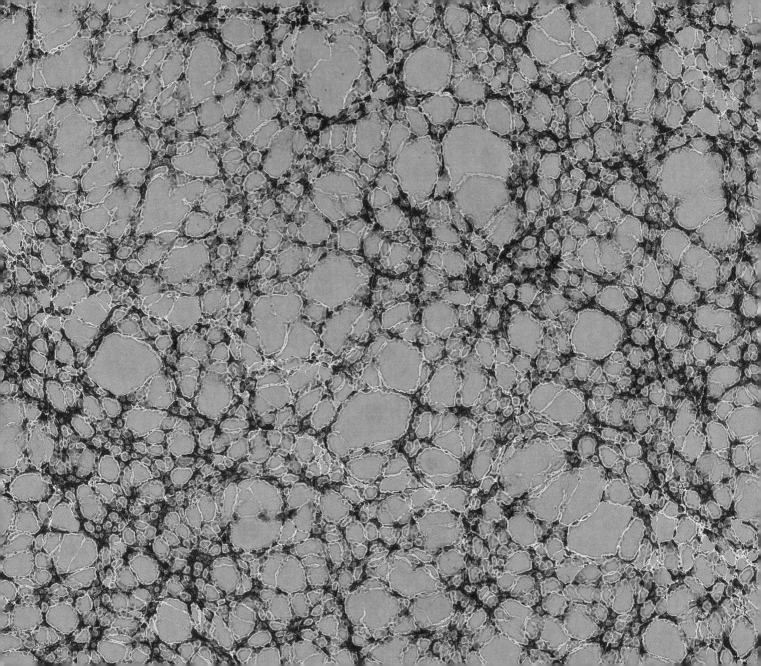